CW00644701

HONEY

HONEY

A BOOK OF RECIPES

HELEN SUDELL

LORENZ BOOKS

First published in 2015 by Lorenz Books
an imprint of Anness Publishing Limited
108 Great Russell Street, London WC1B 3NA
www.annesspublishing.com
www.lorenzbooks.com; info@anness.com

© 2015 Anness Publishing Limited

If you like the images in this book and would like to investigate
using them for publishing, promotions or advertising, please visit
our website www.practicalpictures.com for more information

A CIP catalogue record for this book is available from
The British Library

Publisher: Joanna Lorenz
Editorial Director: Helen Sudell
Designer: Nigel Partridge
Illustrations: Anna Koska
Production Controller: Pirong Wang

Photographers: Martin Brigdale, Craig Robertson, Nicki Dowey,
William Lingwood, Jon Whitaker, Gus Filgate

Printed and bound in China

PUBLISHER'S NOTE
Although the advice and information in this book are believed to
be accurate and true at the time of going to press, neither the
authors nor the publisher can accept any legal responsibility or
liability for any errors or omissions that may have been made nor
for any inaccuracies nor for any loss, harm or injury that comes
about from following instructions or advice in this book.

COOK'S NOTES
• Bracketed terms are intended for American readers.

• For all recipes, quantities are given in both metric and imperial
measures and, where appropriate, in standard cups and spoons.
Follow one set of measures, but not a mixture, because they are
not interchangeable.

• Standard spoon and cup measures are level. 1 tsp = 5ml,
1 tbsp = 15ml, 1 cup = 250ml/8fl oz.

• Australian standard tablespoons are 20ml. Australian readers
should use 3 tsp in place of 1 tbsp for measuring small quantities.

• American pints are 16fl oz/2 cups. American readers should use
20fl oz/2.5 cups in place of 1 pint when measuring liquids.

• Electric oven temperatures in this book are for conventional
ovens. When using a fan oven, the temperature will probably need
to be reduced by about 10–20°C/20–40°F. Since ovens vary, you
should check with your manufacturer's instruction book for
guidance.

• The nutritional analysis given for each recipe is calculated per
portion (i.e. serving or item), unless otherwise stated. If the recipe
gives a range, such as Serves 4–6, then the nutritional analysis will
be for the smaller portion size, i.e. 6 servings. The analysis does not
include optional ingredients, such as salt added to taste.

• Medium (US large) eggs are used unless otherwise stated.

CONTENTS

INTRODUCTION

Honey is one of the oldest foods in existence. It has been used for thousands of years in food and drink as well as beauty products and natural remedies. It has been called liquid gold, the golden elixir and the gift of the gods. For centuries, man has harvested honey, revelling in its sweetness and marvelling at its therapeutic qualities.

The earliest hives were probably accidental – the result of bees nesting in hollow trees, logs or pots – but honey

Below: Crusty bread and honey are a great start to the day.

hunters soon discovered that by trapping the queen in a container of their own making they could have ready access to the delicious sweet treat.

The ancient Egyptians were proficient beekeepers, even moving their hives down the Nile as the flowers that furnished the nectar came into bloom. They fed honey cakes to their sacred animals and used honey in many of their rituals, including the burial of a pharaoh.

A WONDER INGREDIENT

Honey's sweetness is highly prized and has been through the ages. When the Aztecs found their chocolate a little too bitter, they simply stirred in a little honey. The ancient Greeks and Romans used it to make bread and cakes, and the French found honey the perfect sweetener for their famous *pain d'épices*. In Germany it surfaced as *lebkuchen*, while the Italians mixed it with nuts, cocoa,

Above: A worker bumblebee gathers pollen and nectar, and in the process pollinates the flowers that it visits.

spices, and candied peel to make *panforte*. Today, it is as popular as an ingredient in savoury dishes, including marinades and glazes for poultry and meat, salad dressings, and casseroles.

Honey is also prized for its healing properties and is recognized to have antiseptic and antibacterial properties, which can be exploited in many natural remedies.

DIFFERENT FORMS OF HONEY

There are lots of different ways in which honey is sold. You can choose from fresh honeycomb, cut comb, heat-treated honey, set honey or organic honey.

Honeycomb is the bees' own packaging system. This was how most people enjoyed honey but today it is quite difficult to obtain. If offered for sale, it must be fresh from the hive, and not contain any eggs or larvae.

Cut comb or chunk honey is liquid honey with pieces of honeycomb added to the jar. Acacia honey, which is mild and light, is often used as a base.

Liquid honey is the most popular form of honey, and the most versatile. When honey is extracted from the comb, it naturally retains some particles of wax, along with propolis (a resin-like substance taken from certain trees) and pollen grains. These substances give the honey a cloudy appearance. To counter this, beekeepers filter honey through fine mesh.

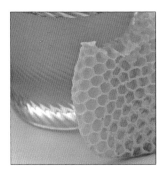

Above: Honey comes in many forms, such as this clear honey and honeycomb.

Pasteurized or heat-treated honey is available, although in health terms there is no reason why honey should be pasteurized as the high sugar content protects against the growth of bacteria.

Set honey is the term applied to any honey that has been solidified through the crystallization of the sugars it contains. This natural process happens faster in some types of honey than others, usually when there is a high proportion of glucose. Honey that has

crystallized spontaneously can be liquified if it is warmed gently. Do not let it get too hot or nutrients will be destroyed.

Creamed honey (also known as spun, whipped, churned or honey fondant) has been deliberately crystallized in controlled conditions so that it forms a smooth mixture. Honey that is high in glucose is ideal for creaming and results in a spreading consistency.

Organic honey is subject to strict guidelines and the beehives must be on land that has been certified organic.

Below: Creamed honey has a smooth, thick texture.

TYPES OF HONEY

There are many types of honey on the market, and although the differences are subtle, honey is just as varied as jam, so it is well worth trying out a range of varieties. Listed below are just a few of the most popular honeys.

Acacia honey is a pale yellow honey with a mild, sweet floral flavour with hints of vanilla. Slow to liquidize, it is a good honey for cooking as it mixes easily in liquids, such as drinks or batters. Cut honeycomb is often placed in jars of acacia honey, since its clarity and pale colour

Below: European acacia honey.

allow the comb to be seen to advantage. It is often blended with other types of honey.

Alfalfa honey is a very pale, almost white honey which is popular in parts of the United States. It has a delicate flavour with a slight spiciness, which makes it a useful ingredient for dressings and sauces.

Clover honey is a white or straw-coloured honey with a mild, butterscotch flavour. Clover honey granulates quickly, so is generally creamed or whipped. It is good for spreading on crumpets or toast and is wonderful in a banana smoothie. New Zealand, Canada and the United States are major producers.

Eucalyptus honey is a clear honey mainly produced in Australia where there are more than 500 varieties of the eucalyptus tree, all of them popular with bees. The honey has a fruity flavour, redolent of raisins, with a toffee aftertaste.

Heather honey is possibly the best-known variety of honey in the world with the finest heather honey coming from Scotland. Depending on its source, it ranges in colour from golden to a rich port-wine shade (bell heather honey). It has a delicious flowery taste. As with good red wine, the flavour of heather honey is said to improve with keeping.

Lavender honey is golden in colour, with a delicate flavour. It is sweet but relatively subtle, making it a good choice for cooking as it will not dominate.

Below: Eucalyptus honey.

Above: Heather honey.

Lime/Linden/Basswood honey are all types of honey from species of the *Tilia* tree. It is a superb honey that is very versatile in the kitchen. The colour – water white to pale yellow – is not particularly exciting, but the aroma is lovely. The flavour has been likened to that of green apples with a touch of mint.

Orange blossom honey is a very popular honey. The colour ranges from white to pale amber and it has a lovely citrus perfume and flavour. It works well in marinades, meat glazes and as a drizzle for roasted vegetables, and is a favourite topping for ice cream, porridge, and crêpes.

Thyme honey has a robust herbal flavour. It is golden in colour with a reddish tinge. The most famous thyme honey is Hymettus, named after a mountain in ancient Greece whose thyme bushes produced honey of such quality that it was called food of the gods.

Tulepo honey is a favourite American honey, golden in colour with a greenish cast. It is much sought-after because of its lovely floral perfume and complex fruity flavour and aftertaste. It has a high rate of fructose so is slow to crystallize.

Below: Thyme honey.

FLAVOURED HONEY
To make flavoured honey at home, choose a base honey with a mild flavour. Pour 450g/1lb honey into a heavy pan, stir in your chosen ingredient (see below) and heat gently for 10 minutes. Do not let the honey approach boiling point. Remove from the heat, cover and leave to stand for 2 hours. Strain the honey into a clean jar, cover and label. **Spice**: add 15ml/1 tbsp allspice berries. **Citrus**: add 15ml/1 tbsp grated orange or lemon rind. **Ginger**: add a 5cm/2in knob fresh ginger, peeled and thinly sliced.

COOKING WITH HONEY

Honey sees us through the day. Many people wake up to a warm drink of tea with honey, or just honey and lemon juice in hot water. At breakfast, honey not only tops cereals, but is also drizzled on muffins and pancakes or simply spread on toast. Honey is often used to sweeten breads and is good in wholemeal (whole-wheat) rolls and loaves.

In a savoury setting, honey makes a delicious vinaigrette. It can also be used as a glaze on roasted vegetables, giving them a lovely flavour and colour. It is particularly good with pumpkin or butternut squash. Honey roast ham is an old favourite, but honey also goes with lamb chops (try mixing it with soy sauce first) and chicken and is delicious as a marinade for barbecued meat. You can even use honey with fish: honey and salmon is a winning combination, and it also tastes great with other fish such as trout or mackerel.

Above: There are numerous shades of honey to choose from.

Below: Citrus-infused honey is light and refreshing.

MEASURING HONEY
If you are measuring honey by the tablespoon, heat the spoon first and the honey will slide off easily. If measuring in a cup, grease the cup first. For larger amounts, weigh the mixing bowl and note its weight, then pour in the honey until it is the required weight.

BUYING HONEY
There are hundreds of types of honey with different colours and flavourings so it is worth experimenting to find the ones you like best. In general, dark honeys have a more intense taste than pale ones. They also tend to have higher levels of antioxidants. If you've always bought honey based on texture (clear or creamed) rather than taste, give yourself a treat by sampling a selection.

STORING HONEY

Store honey in a cool, dry place. It will keep almost indefinitely if the lid is tightly closed.

Do not store honey in the refrigerator. The exception is borage or viper's bugloss honey, which becomes toffee-like when chilled, and kept in the refrigerator for that reason.

BAKING WITH HONEY

Honey is sweeter than sugar, so you need around a third less by volume to achieve the same result. Honey also contains water, so when baking, you need to reduce the amount of other liquids used by about a fifth. A cake recipe might suggest adding a small amount of extra flour, with a raising agent such as bicarbonate of soda (baking soda) to offset the extra liquid. The bicarbonate of soda also neutralizes honey's natural acidity, and helps to make the mixture rise.

An important attribute of honey is that it is hygroscopic, so not only does it contain

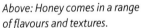

USING HONEY INSTEAD OF SUGAR

To substitute honey for sugar when baking, use 225g/8oz honey for every 200g/7oz/1 cup sugar. Reduce the amount of liquid by 60ml/4tbsp. Beat the mixture well, or dissolve the honey in milk. Reduce the oven temperature: if a cake would normally be baked at 180°C/350°F/Gas 4, lower the temperature to 170°C/325°F/Gas 3.

Above: Honey comes in a range of flavours and textures.

water, but it also attracts liquid. This is useful in baking, since it means that cakes keep moist and fresh. Cakes that have been sweetened with honey look good because their surfaces become golden brown on baking. Avoid over-browning by reducing the oven temperature.

If you are baking and need a mild honey, choose an all-purpose variety like blossom honey or try lavender honey.

Generally, clear honey is easy to use for baking, but a creamy honey would also work.

Honey can be used to sweeten sorbets and ice creams, and is good in fruit ices or mixtures flavoured with nuts. However, because honey freezes at a lower temperature than sugar, the texture will be different. When making a sugar syrup as the basis for a water ice, use a mixture of honey and caster (superfine) sugar.

HONEY DRESSINGS, MARINADES AND GLAZES

Honey is surprisingly delicious in salad dressings, adding a sweet touch that complements many ingredients. It is also excelling as a marinade or glaze, when it adds a unique flavour and glossy stickiness to roasted or barbecued meat, poultry and even fruits.

HONEY AND MUSTARD DRESSING

This tangy dressing gives a kick to a tuna, pasta and corn salad.

In a bowl, mix 60ml/4tbsp extra virgin olive oil, 15ml/ 1 tbsp balsamic vinegar, 5ml/ 1 tsp red wine vinegar, and 5ml/1 tsp Dijon mustard with

10ml/2 tsp clear honey. Add to the salad and toss well to mix.

HONEY AND HERB DRESSING

Mixed herbs, honey, oil and lemon are a perfect foil for a spicy sausage salad.

Mix 30ml/1 tbsp lemon juice, 15ml/1 tbsp clear honey, 90ml/6 tbsp olive oil, 10ml/ 2 tsp French mustard, 30ml/ 2 tbsp chopped fresh herbs, such as coriander (cilantro), chives and parsley. Pour over the salad and serve.

HONEY AND ORANGE MARINADE

A spicy honey and citrus coating ensures that poultry is moist and succulent.

Combine the juice and grated rind of 2 oranges, 2 crushed garlic cloves, 15ml/1 tbsp chopped root ginger, 45ml/ 3 tbsp soy sauce, 75ml/5 tbsp honey and 2–3 star anise with 30ml/2 tbsp rice wine.

Toss the chicken pieces in the marinade, working it in well with your hands so that the meat is thoroughly coated. Chill for 6 hours, or overnight, for a really great flavour.

HONEY AND GINGER MARINADE

Ginger, sour plum sauce and honey are natural partners in this tasty marinade. It tastes equally good with chicken or pork dishes.

In a mortar and pestle grind 6 chopped shallots, 4 chopped garlic cloves and 25g/1oz grated root ginger to a smooth paste. Beat in 30ml/1 tbsp honey; 30ml/2 tbsp each tomato ketchup and sour plum sauce and 15ml/1 tbsp sesame oil.

Toss the meat in the marinade and chill for at least 6 hours. Reserve the marinade and warm through before pouring over the cooked dish just before serving.

HONEY AND SOY GLAZE

Mixed with soy sauce, honey adds a sticky sweet and sour flavour to ribs. They taste wonderful barbecued over hot coals or baked in the oven.

Mix together 75ml/5 tbsp clear honey with 75ml/5 tbsp light soy sauce. Pour or brush over pork spare ribs, turning them several times to ensure they are thoroughly coated. Set aside in the refrigerator to allow the meat to absorb the glaze.

Bake the ribs for 30 minutes at 190°C/375°F/Gas 5, then increase the oven temperature to 220°C/425°F/Gas 7 until there is a thick, sticky glaze on the ribs.

HONEY AND SESAME DIP

Sesame, lemon and honey combine with mint to make a sweet and tangy dip that is wonderful served simply with chunks of crusty fresh bread or toasted pitta bread.

Beat 15ml/3 tbsp light sesame paste with the juice of 1 lemon. Add 30ml/ 2 tbsp clear honey and 5–10ml/1–2 tsp dried mint and beat again until the mixture is thick and creamy. Spoon into a small dish and serve at room temperature with lemon wedges for squeezing.

HONEY DRINKS

Honey adds sweetness and sustenance to drinks, whether hot or cold.

HONEY AND STRAWBERRY SMOOTHIE
This energizing blend is packed with goodness. It contains honey for energy and tofu, which is full of nutrients, as well as vitamin-rich strawberries.

Makes 2 glasses
Put 250g/9oz firm tofu, 200g/7oz/1¾ cups strawberries, juice of 2 large oranges and 1 lemon into a food processor or blender and blend until smooth,

scraping the mixture down the sides of the bowl. Add 15ml/1 tbsp honey and process again until the mixture is thoroughly blended. Divide the smoothie into 2 large glasses and top each glass with a few reserved strawberries and sprinkle with a few pumpkin seeds.

RASPBERRY AND OATMEAL SMOOTHIE
Oatmeal and honey give substance and a little sweetness to this smoothie. Make it ahead so the oats are easier to digest.

Makes 1 large glass
Spoon 25ml/1½ tbsp medium oatmeal into a heatproof bowl. Pour in 120ml/4floz/½ cup boiling water and stand for 10 minutes. Put the oats in a food processor or blender and add 150g/5oz/1 cup raspberries, 10ml/2 tsp honey and 30ml/2 tbsp natural (plain) yogurt. Process until smooth and thick.

Pour into a glass and add a little more yogurt on top and finish with a few raspberries.

SPICED HONEY DRINK
A wonderfully warming drink, perfect for a winter's evening by an open fire.

Makes 1 litre/1¾ pints/4 cups
Put a pinch of ground ginger and 2.5ml/½ tsp ground cinnamon in a medium pan with 500ml/17fl oz/2 cups water and bring to the boil. Lower the heat, cover and simmer for 5 minutes. Set aside. Meanwhile, mix

75g/3oz/¼ cup honey and 50g/2oz/¼ cup sugar in a separate pan. Add the water to the honey and sugar mixture and bring to the boil, constantly stirring. Lower the heat, simmer for 10 minutes, making sure that it does not boil. Serve warm.

TEQUILA SUNSET

This colourful cocktail drink is sure to get any party going with a swing .

Makes 4 cocktails

Pour 25ml/1½ tbsp gold tequila, 120ml/4floz lemon juice and 25ml/1½ tbsp orange juice into a well-chilled cocktail

glass. Mix the ingredients well. Trickle 30ml/2 tbsp clear honey into the centre of the drink. It will sink and create a layer at the bottom of the glass. Add 15ml/1 tbsp creme de cassis, but do not stir. It will create a glowing layer above the honey at the bottom of the glass.

ATHOLL BROSE

This traditional Scottish drink makes good use of heather honey and highland whisky.

Makes 4 small glasses

Place 200g/7oz/2 cups medium rolled oats in a small bowl with 150ml/4fl oz/⅔ cup water and leave for 1 hour, then stir to make a paste. Press the rolled oats complete with the soaking water through a sieve (strainer) into a bowl. Add 120ml/4fl oz/½ cup heather honey and mix until combined. Pour in 900ml/1½ pints/3¾ cups whisky a little at a time, stirring. Pour into small glasses and serve. Keep the drink in bottles and shake before use.

BLAS MEALA

This classic Irish recipe is even more like a dessert that Gaelic coffee. It is debatable whether it should be drunk or eaten with a spoon!

Makes 1 tall glass

In a small pan, heat 50ml/ 2fl oz/¼ cup freshly squeezed orange juice to just below boiling point, then add 5ml/ 1 tsp honey and stir.

Pour into a glass, add 25ml/1½ tbsp Irish whiskey and top with a layer of whipped cream. Sprinkle with a pinch of toasted pinhead oatmeal and drink straight away.

APPETIZERS AND SIDES

BEGIN YOUR DINNER PARTY WITH GRILLED

OYSTERS OOZING WITH HONEY, OR SUCCULENT

CHICKEN WINGS WITH.A HONEY GLAZE, OR PEP

UP YOUR ROAST PARSNIPS WITH A WINNING

COMBINATION OF HONEY AND NUTMEG.

CHINESE CHICKEN WINGS

Lemon is frequently used for marinades in Chinese cuisine. Here it combines with ginger, honey, chilli and garlic to give roasted chicken wings an exotic flavour.

Serves 4

12 chicken wings
3 garlic cloves, crushed
4cm/1½in piece fresh root ginger, peeled and grated
juice of 1 large lemon
45ml/3 tbsp soy sauce
45ml/3 tbsp clear honey
2.5ml/½ tsp chilli powder
150ml/¼ pint/⅔ cup chicken stock
salt and ground black pepper
lemon and lime wedges, to garnish

Remove the wing tips (pinions) and discard. Cut the wings into two pieces. Put the chicken pieces into a shallow dish, cover and set aside.

Mix together the garlic, ginger, lemon and soy sauce. Blend in the honey, chilli powder, seasoning and chicken stock. Pour the mixture over the chicken wings and coat completely. Marinate overnight.

Preheat the oven to 220°C/425°F/Gas 7. Remove the chicken wings from the marinade and arrange them in a single layer in a large roasting pan. Roast for about 25 minutes, generously basting at least twice with the marinade during cooking.

Place the wings on a serving plate. Add the remaining marinade to the roasting pan and bring to the boil. Cook until it turns a syrupy consistency and spoon a little over the wings. Serve the chicken wings immediately, garnished with the lemon and lime wedges.

Energy 622Kcal/2605kJ; Protein 64g;
Carbohydrate 16g, of which sugars 14g;
Fat 34g, of which saturates 12g;
Cholesterol 218mg; Calcium 78mg;
Fibre 0g; Sodium 200mg.

GRILLED OYSTERS WITH HIGHLAND HEATHER HONEY

Heather honey is very fragrant, the pollen gathered by bees late in the season when the heather on the moors is in full flower. It creates a stunning starter with these rich fresh oysters.

Serves 4

*1 bunch spring onions
(scallions), washed
20ml/4 tsp heather honey
10ml/2 tsp soy sauce
16 fresh oysters*

Energy 81kcal/343kJ; Protein 9.2g;
Carbohydrate 9.1g, of which sugars 6.9g;
Fat 1.2g, of which saturates 0.2g;
Cholesterol 46mg; Calcium 121mg; Fibre
0.3g; Sodium 588mg.

Preheat the grill (broiler) to medium. Chop the spring onions finely, removing any coarser outer leaves.

Place the heather honey and soy sauce in a bowl and mix. Then add the finely chopped spring onions and mix them in thoroughly.

Open the oysters with an oyster knife or a small, sharp knife, taking care to catch the liquid in a small bowl. Leave the oysters attached to one side of the shell. Strain the liquid to remove any pieces of broken shell, and set aside.

Place a large teaspoon of the honey and spring onion mixture on top of each oyster.

Place under the preheated grill until the mixture bubbles, which will take about 5 minutes. Take care when removing the oysters from the grill as the shells retain the heat. Make sure that you don't lose any of the sauce from inside the oyster shells.

Allow the oysters to cool slightly before serving with slices of bread to soak up the juices. Either tip them straight into your mouth or lift them out with a spoon or fork.

HONEY-COATED FRITTERS

The ingredients for these very sticky, honey-coated Calabrian party snacks could not be simpler to make, but they are pretty to look at and delicious to eat.

Makes about 30

*500ml/17fl oz/generous 2 cups
  cold water*
*500g/1¼lb/5 cups very fine
  plain (all-purpose) white
  flour or cake flour, sifted
  twice*
light olive oil for deep-frying
90ml/6 tbsp clear honey

COOK'S TIP

It is important to stir constantly while the flour mixture cooks, to prevent lumps from forming. The paste must be smooth.

  Serve the fritters with a dish of orange wedges, which will cut the intense sweetness of the honey.

Energy 103kcal/431kJ; Protein 1.6g;
Carbohydrate 13g, of which sugars 0.3g;
Fat 5.3g, of which saturates 0.8g;
Cholesterol 0mg; Calcium 23mg; Fibre
0.5g; Sodium 1mg.

Pour the water into a heavy pan and bring it to the boil. Gradually trickle in the flour, stirring constantly. Continue to stir until the mixture forms a dough and comes away from the sides of the pan. Turn the dough into a bowl and leave to cool completely.

Pinch off small pieces of dough and roll them into small sausage shapes, each about 5cm/2in long and 5mm/¼in wide. Squeeze each sausage in the middle to make a bow shape.

Heat the oil in a large pan until a small piece of bread dropped into it sizzles instantly.

Add the dough shapes, in batches, and fry until they rise to the surface of the oil and turn golden and crisp.

As each batch cooks, lift the bows out with a slotted spoon and drain on kitchen paper. Place them on a warmed heatproof platter and keep them warm while cooking the remaining shapes.

Heat the honey in a small pan. When it bubbles, pour it all over the fritters.

Allow to cool slightly, but serve while warm.

ROAST PARSNIPS WITH HONEY AND NUTMEG

The Romans considered parsnips to be a luxury, at which time they were credited with a variety of medicinal qualities. Today, they are especially enjoyed when roasted around a joint of beef.

Serves 4–6

4 medium parsnips
30ml/2 tbsp plain (all-purpose) flour seasoned with salt and pepper
60ml/4 tbsp oil
15–30ml/1–2 tbsp clear honey
freshly grated nutmeg

Preheat the oven to 200°C/400°F/Gas 6. Peel the parsnips and cut each one lengthways into quarters, removing any woody cores. Drop into a pan of boiling water and cook for 5 minutes until slightly softened.

Drain the parsnips thoroughly, then toss in the seasoned flour, shaking off any excess.

Pour the oil into a roasting pan and put into the oven until hot. Add the parsnips, tossing them in the oil and arranging them in a single layer. Return the pan to the oven and cook the parsnips for about 30 minutes, turning occasionally, until crisp, golden brown and cooked through.

Drizzle with the honey and sprinkle over a little grated nutmeg. Return the parsnips to the oven for 5 minutes before serving.

Energy 230kcal/956kJ; Protein 2.3g;
Carbohydrate 16.8g, of which sugars 5.1g;
Fat 17.6g, of which saturates 2.1g;
Cholesterol 0mg; Calcium 47mg; Fibre
4.3g; Sodium 9mg

HONEYED ARTICHOKE HEARTS

In this simple summer dish globe artichokes are cooked in a honey dressing with ginger and preserved lemons. They make a good accompaniment to barbecued meat.

Serves 4
30–45ml/2–3 tbsp olive oil
2 garlic cloves, crushed
scant 5ml/1 tsp ground ginger
pinch of saffron threads
juice of ½ lemon
15–30ml/1–2 tbsp honey
peel of 1 preserved lemon, finely
    sliced
8 artichoke hearts, quartered
150ml/¼ pint/⅔ cup water
salt

Energy 142Kcal/586kJ; Protein 1.6g;
Carbohydrate 4.1g, of which sugars 1.9g;
Fat 11.3g, of which saturates 1.6g;
Cholesterol 0mg; Calcium 40mg; Fibre
1.6g; Sodium 47mg.

Heat the olive oil in a heavy pan and add the garlic. Before the garlic begins to colour, stir in the ginger, saffron, lemon juice, honey and preserved lemon peel. Add the artichokes and toss them in the spices and honey. Add the water and a pinch of salt and heat until simmering.

Cover the pan and simmer for 10–15 minutes. If the liquid has not reduced, take the lid off the pan and boil for 2 minutes until it is reduced to a coating consistency. Serve warm.

FISH, POULTRY AND MEAT DISHES

ALTHOUGH WE TEND TO THINK OF HONEY IN

TERMS OF SWEET DISHES, IT MAKES A GREAT

ADDITION TO ALL SORTS OF SAVOURIES,

INCLUDING ROAST GAMMON, SALMON WITH

HONEY AND MUSTARD SAUCE, MOROCCAN LAMB,

AND DUCK WITH HONEYED POTATOES.

ROASTED SALMON WITH HONEY AND MUSTARD

*Baked salmon is a very simple dish to put together but tastes fabulous. The sweet and tangy dressing
cuts through the richness of the fish.*

Serves 4
30ml/2 tbsp olive oil
15ml/1 tbsp honey
*30ml/2 tbsp wholegrain
   mustard*
grated rind ½ lemon
*4 salmon fillets, each about
   150g/5oz*
salt and ground black pepper

To make the marinade, put the oil, honey, mustard and lemon rind in
a small bowl and mix together. Season the marinade with salt and
pepper to taste.

Put the salmon fillets in an ovenproof dish or on a baking sheet lined
with baking parchment and spread the marinade over the each fillet.
Leave to marinate for 30 minutes.

Preheat the oven to 200°C/400°F/Gas 6. Roast the fish in the oven
for 10–12 minutes, until the flesh flakes easily. Serve hot.

Energy 296kcal/1231kJ; Protein 25.9g;
Carbohydrate 3.2g, of which sugars 3.2g;
Fat 20g, of which saturates 3.2g;
Cholesterol 63mg; Calcium 36mg; Fibre
0.4g; Sodium 178mg.

SMOKED FISH PLATTER WITH HONEY DRESSING

A wide variety of smoked fish is available today – trout, salmon and mackerel feature in this simple appetizer – but any smoked fish can be used. Ask your local fishmonger for the best buys.

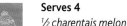

Serves 4

½ charentais melon
½ cantaloupe melon
50g/2oz rocket (arugula)
75g/3oz hot-smoked trout
*   fillets*
75g/3oz smoked salmon
75g/3oz smoked mackerel
*   with peppercorns*

For the dressing

75ml/5 tbsp extra virgin olive oil
15ml/1 tbsp white wine vinegar
5ml/1 tsp wholegrain mustard
5ml/1 tsp clear honey
salt and ground black pepper

Scoop out and discard all the seeds from the charentais and cantaloupe melons and cut each melon into four or eight slices, leaving the skin on. Divide the melon slices among four small serving plates, placing the slices neatly to one side.

Add a quarter of the rocket leaves to each plate, placing them opposite the melon.

Make the honey dressing by combining all the ingredients in a small bowl. Add plenty of salt and black pepper and whisk with a fork until emulsified.

Divide the smoked fish into four portions, breaking or cutting the trout fillets and smoked salmon into bitesize pieces. Peel the skin from the mackerel, then break up the flesh. Arrange the trout fillets, smoked salmon and mackerel over the rocket and melon on each platter. Drizzle the dressing over and serve immediately.

Energy 200kcal/832kJ; Protein 9.7g;
Carbohydrate 8.3g, of which sugars 8.3g;
Fat 14.5g, of which saturates 2.3g;
Cholesterol 22mg; Calcium 39mg; Fibre 0.9g;
Sodium 654mg.

HONEY MUSTARD CHICKEN

Chicken thighs have a rich flavour, but if you want to cut down on fat, use four chicken breast portions instead and cook for 20–25 minutes. Serve with a chunky tomato and red onion salad.

Serves 4

8 chicken thighs
60ml/4 tbsp wholegrain
* mustard*
60ml/4 tbsp clear honey
salt and ground black pepper

Preheat the oven to 1900C/3750F/Gas 5. Put the chicken thighs in a single layer in a roasting pan.

Mix together the mustard and honey, season with salt and ground black pepper to taste and brush the mixture all over the chicken thighs.

Cook for 25–30 minutes, brushing the chicken with the pan juices occasionally, until cooked through. (To check the chicken is cooked through, skewer it with a sharp knife; the juices should run clear.)

Energy 244Kcal/1028kJ; Protein 27g;
Carbohydrate 12g, of which sugars 12g;
Fat 10g, of which saturates 2g;
Cholesterol 130mg; Calcium 33mg;
Fibre 0.7g; Sodium 400mg.

GARLIC-ROASTED QUAILS WITH HONEY

This is a great Indo-Chinese favourite made with quails or poussins. Crispy, tender and juicy, they are simple to prepare and delicious to eat. Roast them in the oven or over a barbecue.

Serves 4

150ml/¼ pint/⅔ cup mushroom soy sauce
45ml/3 tbsp honey
15ml/1 tbsp sugar
8 garlic cloves, crushed
15ml/1 tbsp black peppercorns, crushed
30ml/2 tbsp sesame oil
8 quails or poussins
nuoc cham (fish sauce), *to serve*

USING CHICKEN
If you can't find quails or poussins, you could easily improvise by making it with whole chicken legs instead. The results will be just as good, and the cooking times similar.

Energy 649Kcal/2701kJ; Protein 51g; Carbohydrate 17g, of which sugars 3g; Fat 43g, of which saturates 11g; Cholesterol 250mg; Calcium 61mg; Fibre 0.2g; Sodium 0.2g

In a bowl, beat the mushroom soy sauce with the honey and sugar until the sugar has dissolved. Stir in the garlic, crushed peppercorns and sesame oil. Put the quails or poussins into a flat dish and rub the marinade over them with your fingers. Cover and chill for at least 4 hours.

Preheat the oven to 230°C/450°F/Gas 8. Place the quails breast side down in a roasting pan or on a wire rack set over a baking tray, then put them in the oven for 10 minutes.

Take them out and turn them over so they are breast side up, baste well with the juices and return them to the oven for a further 15–20 minutes. Serve immediately with *nuoc cham* for dipping or drizzling over the meat.

ROASTED DUCKLING ON A BED OF HONEYED POTATOES

The rich flavour of duck combined with these sweetened potatoes glazed with honey makes an excellent course for a dinner party or special occasion.

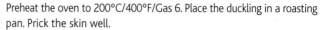

Serves 4

1 duckling, giblets removed
60ml/4 tbsp light soy sauce
150ml/¼ pint/⅔ cup fresh
  orange juice
3 large floury potatoes, cut
  into chunks
30ml/2 tbsp clear honey
15ml/1 tbsp sesame seeds
salt and ground black pepper

Preheat the oven to 200°C/400°F/Gas 6. Place the duckling in a roasting pan. Prick the skin well.

Mix the soy sauce and orange juice together and pour over the duck. Cook for 20 minutes.

Place the potato chunks in a bowl and stir in the honey, then toss to mix well. Remove the duckling from the oven and spoon the potatoes all around and under the duckling.

Roast for 35 minutes and remove from the oven. Toss the potatoes in the juices so the underside will be cooked and turn the duck over. Put back in the oven and cook for a further 30 minutes.

Remove the duckling from the oven and carefully scoop off the excess fat, leaving the juices behind.

Sprinkle the sesame seeds over the potatoes, season and turn the duckling back over, breast side up, and cook for a further 10 minutes. Remove the duckling and potatoes from the oven and keep warm, allowing the duck to stand for a few minutes.

Pour off the excess fat and simmer the juices on the hob for a few minutes. Serve the juices with the carved duckling and potatoes.

Energy 806kcal/3341kJ; Protein 20.8g; Carbohydrate 32.3g, of which sugars 6.4g; Fat 66.8g, of which saturates 17.9g; Cholesterol 0mg; Calcium 53mg; Fibre 2.1g; Sodium 403mg.

HONEY-ROAST HAM

This stunning baked ham is a versatile dish for a family celebration. It can be served hot or cold with a selection of pickles, such as gherkins or beetroot (beet), and horseradish sauce.

Serves 4–6

2.75–3.6kg/6–8lb ham
250ml/8fl oz/1 cup clear honey
20 whole cloves
sweet gherkins, pickled beetroot
*   (beet) and horseradish sauce,*
*   to serve*

For the marinade

1 litre/1¾ pints/4 cups water
250ml/8fl oz/1 cup cider
*   vinegar*
1 onion, sliced
4–5 bay leaves
8 whole cloves
2 cinnamon sticks
8 allspice berries
4–5 dried chillies
5ml/1 tsp yellow mustard seeds
15ml/1 tbsp sugar

To make the marinade, put all the ingredients in a large pan with a lid. Weigh the ham and calculate the cooking time, allowing 20 minutes per 450g/1lb of meat.

Put the ham in the pan, cover with a lid and simmer for 2–2¾ hours, or until the rind on the ham has lifted away from the meat slightly. Remove the meat from the pan.

Preheat the oven to 220°C/425°F/Gas 7. Carefully remove the skin from the ham and discard. Score the fat on the ham with a diamond pattern using a large, sharp knife.

Warm the honey gently in a small pan to make a glaze. Do not boil.

Place the ham in a roasting pan and press a clove into the centre of each diamond. Brush the ham with honey, then place in the oven and roast for 20–25 minutes until the fat is brown and crispy.

Serve hot or cold.

Energy 595kcal/2482kJ; Protein 68g;
Carbohydrate 0g, of which sugars 0g; Fat
35.9g, of which saturates 12g; Cholesterol
242mg; Calcium 26mg; Fibre 0g; Sodium
3442mg

MOROCCAN LAMB WITH HONEY AND PRUNES

This dish is eaten by Moroccan Jews at Rosh Hashanah, when sweet foods are traditionally served in anticipation of a prosperous New Year to come.

Serves 6

130g/4½ oz/generous ½ cup pitted prunes
350ml/12fl oz/1½ cups hot tea
1kg/2¼lb stewing or braising lamb, cut into chunky portions
1 onion, chopped
75–90ml/5–6 tbsp chopped fresh parsley
2.5ml/½ tsp ground ginger
2.5ml/½ tsp curry powder or ras al hanout
pinch of freshly grated nutmeg
10ml/2 tsp ground cinnamon
1.5ml/¼ tsp saffron threads
30ml/2 tbsp hot water
75–120ml/5–9 tbsp honey, to taste
250ml/8fl oz/1 cup beef or lamb stock
115g/4oz/1 cup blanched almonds, toasted
30ml/2 tbsp chopped fresh coriander (cilantro) leaves
3 hard-boiled eggs, cut into wedges
salt and ground black pepper

Preheat the oven to 180°C/350°F/Gas 4. Put the prunes in a bowl, pour over the tea and cover. Leave to soak and plump up.

Meanwhile, put the lamb, chopped onion, parsley, ginger, curry powder or ras al hanout, nutmeg, cinnamon, salt and a large pinch of ground black pepper in a roasting pan. Cover and cook in the oven for about 2 hours, or until the meat is tender.

Drain the prunes; add their liquid to the lamb. Combine the saffron and hot water and add to the pan with the honey and stock. Bake, uncovered, for 30 minutes, turning the lamb occasionally.

Add the prunes to the pan and stir gently to mix. Serve sprinkled with the toasted almonds and chopped coriander, and topped with the wedges of hard-boiled egg.

Energy 492kcal/2054kJ; Protein 43.2g; Carbohydrate 17.9g, of which sugars 15.9g; Fat 28.1g, of which saturates 7.6g; Cholesterol 239mg; Calcium 141mg; Fibre 3.9g; Sodium 306mg.

SWEET-AND-SOUR PORK WITH HONEY

Pork fillet is cut in strips before being grilled. Shredded and then tossed with a delicious sweet-sour sauce, it makes a marvellous warm salad.

Serves 4

30ml/2 tbsp dark soy sauce
15ml/1 tbsp clear honey
400g/14oz pork fillet (tenderloin)
6 shallots, very thinly sliced
*   lengthways*
1 lemon grass stalk, thinly sliced
5 kaffir lime leaves, thinly sliced
5cm/2in piece fresh root ginger,
*   sliced*
½ fresh long red chilli, seeded
*   and sliced*
bunch fresh coriander (cilantro),
*   chopped*

For the dressing

30ml/2 tbsp palm sugar
30ml/2 tbsp Thai fish sauce
juice of 2 limes
20ml/4 tsp thick tamarind juice,
*   made by mixing tamarind*
*   paste with warm water*

Energy 170Kcal/718kJ; Protein 22g;
Carbohydrate 12.2g, of which sugars 12.1g;
Fat 4g, of which saturates 1.4g; Cholesterol
63mg; Calcium 16mg; Fibre 0.2g; Sodium
873mg.

Preheat the grill (broiler). Put the soy sauce and the honey in a small bowl and mix well.

Using a sharp knife, cut the pork fillet lengthways into quarters to make four long, thick strips. Place them in a grill (broiling) pan. Brush with the soy sauce and honey mixture, then grill (broil) for about 10–15 minutes, until cooked through. Turn the strips over often and baste with the honey mixture.

Transfer the cooked pork strips to a board. Slice the meat across the grain, then shred it with a fork. Place in a large bowl and add the shallot slices, lemon grass, kaffir lime leaves, ginger, chilli and chopped coriander.

Make the dressing. Place the sugar, fish sauce, lime juice and tamarind juice in a bowl. Whisk until the sugar has completely dissolved. Pour the dressing over the pork mixture and toss well to mix, then serve.

CHILLI AND HONEY-CURED DRIED BEEF

Drying is an ancient method of preserving food, which also intensifies the flavour of some ingredients. The chilli and honey combine to create an irresistible hot-sweet taste.

Serves 4

450g/1lb beef sirloin
2 lemon grass stalks, trimmed
    and chopped
2 garlic cloves, chopped
2 dried Serrano chillies, seeded
    and chopped
30–45ml/2–3 tbsp honey
15ml/1 tbsp nuoc cham *(fish
    sauce)*
30ml/2 tbsp soy sauce
rice wrappers, fresh herbs and
    dipping sauce, to serve
    (optional)

Trim the beef and cut it against the grain into thin, rectangular slices.

Using a mortar and pestle, grind the lemon grass, garlic and chillies to a paste. Stir in the honey, nuoc cham and soy sauce. Put the beef into a bowl, tip in the paste and rub it into the meat.

Arrange the meat on a rack and put it in the refrigerator, uncovered, for 2 days.

Cook the beef on the barbecue or grill and serve with rice wrappers, herbs and a dipping sauce.

Energy 138Kcal/581kJ; Protein 18g;
Carbohydrate 9g, of which sugars 8g; Fat
3g, of which saturates 2g; Cholesterol
38mg; Calcium 7mg; Fibre 0.1g; Sodium
40mg.

CAKES, BAKES AND BREAD

ONE OF HONEY'S MANY ATTRIBUTES IS ITS

ABILITY TO ABSORB LIQUID, SO CAKES AND BAKES

MADE WITH HONEY REMAIN MOIST AND HAVE

EXCELLENT KEEPING QUALITIES. THEY ALSO TASTE

SUPERB, SO YOU MAY NOT GET THE

OPPORTUNITY TO PROVE THE POINT.

WALNUT AND HONEY BARS

A sweet, custard-like filling brimming with walnuts sits on a crisp pastry base. These scrumptious bars are pure heaven to bite into – perfect for a tea-time treat.

Makes 12–14

175g/6oz/1½ cups plain (all-purpose) flour
30ml/2 tbsp icing (confectioners') sugar, sifted
115g/4oz/½ cup unsalted (sweet) butter, diced

For the filling

300g/11oz/scant 3 cups walnut halves
2 eggs, beaten
50g/2oz/¼ cup unsalted (sweet) butter, melted
50g/2oz/¼ cup light muscovado (brown) sugar
90ml/6 tbsp dark clear honey
30ml/2 tbsp single (light) cream

Energy 333kcal/1386kJ; Protein 5.4g;
Carbohydrate 21.4g, of which sugars 11.7g;
Fat 25.7g, of which saturates 7.8g;
Cholesterol 53mg; Calcium 49mg;
Fibre 1.1g; Sodium 85mg

Preheat the oven to 190°C/375°F/Gas 5. Lightly grease a 28 x 18cm/ 11 x 7in shallow tin (pan).

Put the flour, icing sugar and butter in a food processor and process until the mixture forms crumbs. Using the pulse button, add 15–30ml/ 1–2 tbsp water – enough to make a firm dough.

Roll the dough out on baking parchment and line the base and sides of the tin. Trim and fold the top edge inwards.

Prick the base, line with foil and baking beans and bake blind for 10 minutes. Remove the foil and beans. Return the base to the oven for about 5 minutes, until cooked but not browned. Reduce the temperature to 180°C/350°F/Gas 4.

For the filling, sprinkle the walnuts over the base. Whisk the remaining ingredients together. Pour over the walnuts and bake for 25 minutes.

HONEY AND ALMOND COOKIES

These delectable spiced honey cookies originate from Poland where they are traditionally made at Christmas. They are so delicious that they are also eaten at other times of the year.

Makes 20

250ml/8fl oz/1 cup clear honey
4 eggs, plus 2 egg whites
350g/12oz/3 cups plain
  (all-purpose) flour
5ml/1 tsp bicarbonate of soda
  (baking soda)
2.5ml/½ tsp freshly grated
  nutmeg
2.5ml/½ tsp ground ginger
2.5ml/½ tsp ground cinnamon
2.5ml/½ tsp ground cloves
20 blanched almond halves

Beat together the honey and whole eggs until light and fluffy. Sift over the flour, bicarbonate of soda and spices, and beat to combine.

Gather the cookie dough into a ball, wrap in clear film (plastic wrap) and chill in the refrigerator for 1 hour or overnight.

Preheat the oven to 200°C/400°F/Gas 6. Roll out the dough on a lightly floured surface to a thickness of 5mm/¼ in. Using a 4cm/1½ in cookie cutter, stamp out 20 rounds.

Transfer the rounds to two lightly greased baking trays. Beat the egg whites until soft peaks form. Brush the tops of the rounds with the egg white, then press an almond half into the centre of each one.

Place in the oven and bake for 15–20 minutes, or until they are a pale golden brown.

Remove from the oven and allow to cool slightly before transferring to a wire cooling rack. Leave to cool completely, then serve.

Energy 112kcal/473kJ; Protein 3.4g;
Carbohydrate 22.6g, of which sugars 8.9g;
Fat 1.5g, of which saturates 0.4g;
Cholesterol 38mg; Calcium 33mg; Fibre
0.5g; Sodium 22mg.

HONEY AND SPICE CAKES

These golden little cakes are fragrant with honey and cinnamon. Although they can be cooked directly in a bun tin, they tend to rise higher (and are therefore lighter) when baked in paper cases.

Makes 18

250g/9oz/2 cups plain (all-purpose) flour
5ml/1 tsp ground cinnamon
5ml/1 tsp bicarbonate of soda (baking soda)
125g/4¼oz/½ cup butter, softened
125g/4¼oz/10 tbsp soft (light) brown sugar
1 large (US extra large) egg, separated
120ml/4fl oz/½ cup clear honey
about 60ml/4 tbsp milk
caster (superfine) sugar, for sprinkling

Energy 152kcal/639kJ; Protein 1.9g; Carbohydrate 23.6g, of which sugars 13g; Fat 6.3g, of which saturates 3.8g; Cholesterol 26mg; Calcium 30mg; Fibre 0.4g; Sodium 49mg

Preheat the oven to 200°C/400°F/Gas 6. Butter the holes of a bun tin (pan) or, alternatively, line them with paper cases.

Sift the flour into a large mixing bowl with the cinnamon and the bicarbonate of soda.

Beat the butter with the sugar until light and fluffy. Beat in the egg yolk, then gradually add the honey.

With a large metal spoon and a cutting action, fold in the flour mixture plus sufficient milk to make a soft mixture that will just drop off the spoon.

In a separate bowl whisk the egg white until stiff peaks form. Using a large metal spoon, fold the egg white into the cake mixture.

Divide the mixture among the paper cases or the holes in the prepared tin. Put into the hot oven and cook for 15–20 minutes or until risen, firm to the touch and golden brown.

Sprinkle the tops lightly with caster sugar and leave to cool completely on a wire rack.

HONEY AND YOGURT MUFFINS

These filling and substantial wholemeal breakfast muffins are made with honey rather than with sugar, so are not overly sweet. Try a few varieties of honey to see which you prefer.

Makes 12 standard muffins

55g/2oz/¼ cup butter
75ml/5 tbsp clear honey
250ml/8fl oz/1 cup natural (plain) yogurt
1 egg
grated rind of 1 lemon
65ml/2fl oz lemon juice
150g/5oz/1¼ cups plain (all-purpose) flour
175g/6oz/1½ cups wholemeal (whole-wheat) flour
7.5ml/1½ tsp bicarbonate of soda (baking soda)
pinch of freshly grated nutmeg

Preheat the oven to 190°C/375°F/Gas 5. Line the cups of a muffin tin (pan) with paper cases.

In a small pan, melt the butter and honey over a gentle heat. Stir to combine. Remove from the heat and set aside to cool slightly.

In a bowl, whisk together the yogurt, egg, lemon rind and juice. Add the butter and honey mixture. Set aside.

In another bowl, sift together the dry ingredients.

Fold the dry ingredients into the yogurt mixture to blend, then fill the prepared cups two-thirds full.

Bake until the tops spring back when touched lightly. This should be around 20–25 minutes.

Leave to cool in the tin for 5 minutes before turning out on to a wire rack. Serve warm or at room temperature, drizzled with honey, if you like. Store the cold muffins in an airtight container for up to 3 days.

Energy 155kcal/652kJ; Protein 4.7g; Carbohydrate 25.4g, of which sugars 6.9g; Fat 4.6g, of which saturates 2.5g; Cholesterol 25mg; Calcium 66mg; Fibre 1.7g; Sodium 50mg.

WHOLEMEAL AND SPELT LOAF WITH HONEY

Spelt is an ancient grain that predates modern wheat and so has a lower gluten content. This makes the texture cakier than regular bread. The honey keeps the loaf deliciously moist.

Makes 2 23cm/9in round loaves

200g/7oz mixed seeds (pumpkin, sunflower, sesame, poppy seed)
450g/1lb/4 cups strong wholemeal (whole-wheat) bread flour
450g/1lb/4 cups strong spelt bread flour, brown or white
7.5ml/1½ tsp salt
15g/½oz fresh yeast
600ml/1 pint/2½ cups warm water
30ml/2 tbsp runny honey
butter and honey, to serve

Roughly break up the seeds with a pestle and mortar, or whizz briefly in a food processor or blender.

In a large bowl mix the flours and seeds with the salt and yeast. Add the water and the honey and mix to make a soft dough.

Transfer the dough to a floured board and knead on a flat work surface for 10 minutes, until smooth and shiny. Leave to rise covered with clear film (plastic wrap) in a clean bowl in a warm place for 2–3 hours, until roughly doubled in size.

Divide the dough in half and shape to fit into two 23cm/9in round loaf tins (pans). Leave to rise in a warm place covered with a dish towel for about 1 hour, until risen and puffy. When risen, slash the top of the loaves with a sharp knife to help the bread expand as it bakes.

Meanwhile, preheat the oven to 230°C/450°F/Gas 8. Bake for 15 minutes, then reduce the oven temperature to 200°C/400°F/Gas 6 and bake for a further 25 minutes.

Take the tins out of the oven and turn a loaf of bread out. If it sounds hollow when it is tapped, they are cooked. If not, put them back in the oven, close the door and bake until they do sound hollow. Cool on a wire rack and serve with butter and honey.

Energy 2081kcal/8792kJ; Protein 80g; Carbohydrate 340g, of which sugars 20g; Fat 54g, of which saturates 8g; Cholesterol 0mg; Calcium 442mg; Fibre 28.1g; Sodium 526mg.

HOT AND COLD DESSERTS

SOME OF THE SIMPLEST AND MOST DELICIOUS DESSERTS ARE BASED ON HONEY. WHETHER YOU ARE CRAVING COOLING HONEY-INFUSED ICE CREAM, A FRAGRANT HONEY AND SAFFRON BAKED PEAR OR A TRADITIONAL CREAMY FUDGE, HONEY ENSURES THE SWEET TASTE OF SUCCESS.

LAVENDER AND HONEY ICE CREAM

Honey and lavender make a memorable partnership in this old-fashioned and elegant ice cream.
Serve scooped into glasses or set in little moulds and top with lightly whipped cream.

Serves 6–8

90ml/6 tbsp clear honey
4 egg yolks
10ml/2 tsp cornflour
*   (cornstarch)*
8 lavender sprigs, plus extra, to
*   decorate*
450ml/³⁄₄ pint/scant 2 cups milk
450ml/³⁄₄ pint/scant 2 cups
*   whipping cream*

Energy 308kcal/1275kJ; Protein 4.5g;
Carbohydrate 13.9g, of which sugars 12.8g;
Fat 26.4g, of which saturates 15.6g;
Cholesterol 163mg; Calcium 113mg; Fibre
0g; Sodium 45mg.

Put the honey, egg yolk, and cornflour in a bowl. Separate the lavender flowers and add them plus a little milk. Whisk lightly. In a pan bring the remaining milk to the boil. Add to the egg yolk mixture, stirring well.

Return the mixture to the pan and cook very gently, stirring until the mixture thickens. Pour the custard into a bowl, cover the surface with baking parchment and leave to cool, then chill until very cold.

By hand: Whip the cream and fold into the custard. Pour into a container and freeze for 3–4 hours, beating twice as it thickens. Return to the freezer until ready to serve.

Using an ice cream maker: Stir the cream into the custard, then churn the mixture until it holds its shape. Transfer to a tub or similar freezerproof container and freeze until ready to serve.

Transfer the ice cream to the refrigerator 30 minutes before serving, so that it softens slightly. Serve decorated with lavender flowers.

HONEY PUDDING WITH RICOTTA

This recipe originated on the islands of Madeira and Azores, where it is a very popular dessert. The flavour of the pudding is characterized by the mixture of honey and molasses.

Serves 8
olive oil, for brushing
breadcrumbs, for sprinkling
8 eggs
300g/11oz/1½ cups sugar
50g/2oz/2½ tbsp molasses
50g/2oz/¼ cup clear honey
2.5ml/½ tsp ground cinnamon
5ml/1 tsp dried yeast
ricotta or other fresh cheese, to
  serve

Preheat the oven to 180°C/350°F/Gas 4. Brush 8 40cm/1½in square moulds with a little olive oil and sprinkle with breadcrumbs, shaking out the excess.

Beat the eggs in a bowl, then beat in all the remaining ingredients until well blended.

Divide the mixture among the prepared moulds and place them in a roasting pan. Add sufficient boiling water to come about halfway up the sides of the moulds and bake for about 15 minutes, until risen.

Give the puddings approximately 5 minutes to fully stabilise and then turn them out while they are still warm. Serve with ricotta or other fresh cheese.

Energy 267kcal/1133kJ; Protein 7g; Carbohydrate 50.7g, of which sugars 48.2g; Fat 5.7g, of which saturates 1.6g; Cholesterol 190mg; Calcium 88mg; Fibre 0.1g; Sodium 108mg.

VANILLA, HONEY AND SAFFRON PEARS

These sweet juicy pears poached in a vanilla-, saffron- and lime-infused honey syrup make a truly elegant dessert. For a luxurious treat, serve with cream or ice cream.

Serves 4

*150g/5oz/¾ cup caster
    (superfine) sugar
105ml/7 tbsp clear honey
5ml/1 tsp finely grated lime rind
a large pinch of saffron
2 vanilla pods (beans)
4 large, firm ripe dessert pears
single (light) cream or ice
    cream, to serve (optional)*

COOK'S TIP
For the best result, use firm,
ripe dessert pears such as
comice or conference.

Energy 283kcal/1207kJ; Protein 0.8g;
Carbohydrate 74.3g, of which sugars 74.3g;
Fat 0.2g, of which saturates 0g; Cholesterol
0mg; Calcium 38mg; Fibre 3.3g; Sodium
10mg.

Place the caster sugar and honey in a medium, non-stick pan or wok, then add the lime rind and the saffron. Using a small, sharp knife, split the vanilla pods in half and scrape the seeds into the pan, then add the vanilla pods as well.

Pour 500ml/17fl oz/scant 2¼ cups water into the pan and bring the mixture to the boil. Reduce the heat to low and simmer, stirring occasionally, while you prepare the pears.

Peel the pears, then add to the pan and gently turn in the syrup to coat evenly. Cover the pan and simmer gently for 12–15 minutes, turning the pears halfway through cooking, until they are just tender.

Lift the pears from the syrup using a slotted spoon and transfer to four serving bowls. Set aside.

Bring the syrup back to the boil and cook gently for about 10 minutes, or until reduced and thickened. Spoon the syrup over the pears and serve either warm or chilled.

BAKLAVA

The origins of this recipe are in Greece and Turkey, but it has been willingly adopted throughout south-eastern Europe. It is a very sweet dessert and black coffee is the perfect accompaniment.

Makes 24

175g/6oz/¾ cup butter, melted
400g/14oz packet filo pastry
30ml/2 tbsp lemon juice
60ml/4 tbsp clear thick honey
50g/2oz/¼ cup caster
(superfine) sugar
finely grated rind of 1 lemon
10ml/2 tsp cinnamon
200g/7oz/1¾ cups blanched
almonds, chopped
200g/7oz/1¾ cups walnuts,
chopped
75g/3oz/¾ cup pistachios,
chopped, plus extra to
decorate

For the syrup

350g/12oz/1¾ cups caster
(superfine) sugar
115g/4oz/½ cup clear honey
600ml/1 pint/2½ cups water
2 strips of pared lemon rind

Preheat the oven to 160°C/325°F/Gas 3. Brush the base of a shallow 30 × 20cm/12 × 8in loose-bottomed tin (pan) with a little melted butter.

Using the tin as a guide cut the sheets of filo pastry with a sharp knife to fit the tin exactly.

Place one sheet of pastry in the base of the tin, brush with a little melted butter, then repeat until you have used half of the pastry sheets. Set the remaining pastry aside and cover with a clean dish towel.

To make the filling, place the lemon juice, honey and sugar in a pan and heat gently until dissolved. Stir in the lemon rind, cinnamon and chopped nuts. Mix thoroughly.

Spread half the filling over the pastry, cover with 3 layers of the filo pastry and butter then spread the remaining filling over the pastry.

Finish by using up the remaining sheets of pastry and butter on top, and brush the top of the pastry liberally with butter.

Using a sharp knife, carefully mark the pastry into squares, almost cutting through the filling. Bake in the preheated oven for 1 hour, or until crisp and golden brown.

Meanwhile, make the syrup. Place the caster sugar, honey, water and lemon rind in a pan and stir over a low heat until the sugar and honey have dissolved. Bring to the boil, then boil for a further 10 minutes until the mixture has thickened slightly.

Take the syrup off the heat and leave to cool slightly. Remove the baklava from the oven. Remove and discard the lemon rind from the syrup then pour over the pastry. Leave to soak for 6 hours or overnight. Cut into squares and serve, decorated with chopped pistachios.

Energy 839kcal/3490kJ; Protein 9.2g; Carbohydrate 63.2g, of which sugars 62.6g; Fat 62.8g, of which saturates 20.9g; Cholesterol 77mg; Calcium 105mg; Fibre 2.4g; Sodium 258mg.

FLOWER PETAL RICE CAKES IN HONEY

This gorgeous spring dish from Korea uses edible flower petals to flavour rice cakes, which are then drizzled with honey. Its sophisticated appearance is matched by its refined, exquisite taste.

Serves 4
20 edible flower petals
225g/8oz/2 cups sweet
*   rice flour*
2.5ml/½ tsp salt
vegetable oil, for shallow-frying
30ml/ 2 tbsp clear honey

Rinse the flower petals, and gently pat them dry with kitchen paper.

Sift the flour and salt into a bowl and add 300ml/½ pint/1¼ cups warm water. Mix well and knead for 10 minutes. Place on a lightly floured surface and roll out the dough to 1cm/½in thick. Use a floured 5cm/2in biscuit (cookie) cutter to cut the dough into rounds.

Heat the oil in a frying pan over a low flame. Add the rice cakes and fry for 2 minutes, or until lightly browned. Flip over and cook on the other side, and then remove from the pan. Place on kitchen paper to drain the excess oil, then arrange on a serving platter.

Sprinkle the petals over the rice cakes, and then drizzle with honey.

Energy 255kcal/1065kJ; Protein 3.6g; Carbohydrate 45.1g, of which sugars 0g; Fat 6g, of which saturates 0.7g; Cholesterol 0mg; Calcium 14mg; Fibre 1.1g; Sodium 249mg.

COOK'S TIP
A number of different flowers have edible petals, including roses, azaleas, apple blossom, carnations and chrysanthemums.

PESTIÑOS

Bathed in scented honey syrup, these Spanish puff balls are often deep-fried. However, at home it is easier to bake them and they puff up beautifully in the oven.

Makes about 30

225g/8oz/2 cups plain (all-purpose) flour, plus extra for dusting
60ml/4 tbsp sunflower oil
15ml/1 tbsp aniseed, lightly crushed
45ml/3 tbsp caster (superfine) sugar
250ml/8fl oz/1 cup water
60ml/4 tbsp anisette
3 small (US medium) eggs

For the anis syrup

60ml/4 tbsp clear honey
60ml/4 tbsp anisette

Preheat the oven to 190°C/375°F/Gas 5. Sift the flour on to a sheet of baking parchment. Heat the oil in a small pan with the crushed aniseed, until the aniseed releases its aroma. Strain the oil into a larger pan and add the sugar, water and anisette. Heat to a rolling boil.

Remove the pan from the heat and add the sifted flour, all in one go. Beat vigorously with a wooden spoon until the mixture leaves the sides of the pan clean. Leave to cool.

Meanwhile lightly beat the eggs. Gradually incorporate the egg into the dough mixture, beating hard. You may not need to use all the egg – the paste should be soft but not sloppy. Reserve any remaining beaten egg and set aside.

Grease and flour two baking sheets. Fit a plain nozzle to a piping (pastry) bag and pipe small rounds of dough about 2.5cm/1in across on the sheets, spacing them about 2.5cm/1in apart. Brush with the remaining beaten egg.

Bake for about 30 minutes, or until lightly brown and an even texture right through (lift one off the sheet to test).

Melt the honey in a small pan and stir in the anisette. Just before serving, use a slotted spoon to dunk the pestiños into the syrup.

Energy 65kcal/272kJ; Protein 1.3g; Carbohydrate 8.9g, of which sugars 3.2g; Fat 2.1g, of which saturates 0.3g; Cholesterol 19mg; Calcium 14mg; Fibre 0.2g; Sodium 8mg.

COOK'S TIP

Anisette is a sweet aniseed liqueur that gives the syrup a wonderful flavour. If you cannot find anisette, use another anis spirit such as Ricard instead.

HONEY AND GINGER BAKED APPLES

These spicy baked apples are a perfect excuse to cook in the autumn when apples are plentiful.
A final touch of luxury is to fold a little whipped cream into the sauce just before serving.

Serves 4

4 eating apples, such as Cox's
    Orange Pippin or Golden
    Delicious
30ml/2 tbsp finely chopped
    fresh root ginger
60ml/4 tbsp honey
25g/1oz/2 tbsp unsalted butter
60ml/4 tbsp medium white wine
vanilla sauce, to serve

For the vanilla sauce

300ml/½ pint/1¼ cups single
    (light) cream
1 vanilla pod (bean), split
    lengthways
2 egg yolks
30ml/2 tbsp caster (superfine)
    sugar

To make the vanilla sauce, put the cream and vanilla pod in a pan and heat gently to just below boiling point. Remove from the heat and leave to infuse for 10 minutes. Remove the vanilla pod.

Put the egg yolks and sugar in a bowl and whisk them together until pale and thick, then slowly pour into the cream in a steady stream, whisking all the time. Return the pan to the heat and heat very gently until the cream is thick enough to coat the back of a wooden spoon. (If you draw a finger horizontally across the back of the spoon, the sauce should be thick enough not to run down through the channel.) Remove from the heat and leave to cool. Either stir from time to time or cover to prevent a skin forming.

Preheat the oven to 160°C/325°F Gas 3. Remove the cores from the apples leaving the stalk end intact, but remove the actual stalk. Fill each cavity with 2.5ml/½ tbsp chopped ginger and 15ml/1 tbsp honey.

Place the apples in an ovenproof dish, with the open end uppermost, and top each one with a knob of butter. Pour in the wine and bake in the oven, basting frequently with the cooking juices, for about 45 minutes, until the apples are tender.

Serve the apples with the vanilla sauce.

Energy 331kcal/1381kJ; Protein 4.3g;
Carbohydrate 27.8g, of which sugars 27.8g;
Fat 22.3g, of which saturates 13.2g;
Cholesterol 155mg; Calcium 89mg; Fibre
1.2g; Sodium 68mg.

VANILLA HONEY FUDGE

Always a popular choice, home-made fudge ends a meal beautifully when served as a petit four –
this meltingly good vanilla and honey version is sure to become a favourite.

Makes about 60 pieces
175g/6oz/¾ cup butter
675g/1½lb/3 cups soft light
   brown sugar
400g/14oz can sweetened
   condensed milk
60ml/4 tbsp honey
2.5ml/½ tsp vanilla extract

Energy 103Kcal/435kJ; Protein 0.7g;
Carbohydrate 19.4g, of which sugars 19.4g;
Fat 3.1g, of which saturates 1.9g;
Cholesterol 9mg; Calcium 28mg; Fibre 0g;
Sodium 28mg.

Butter a shallow tin (pan). Warm the butter and 150ml/¼ pint/⅔ cup
water in a heavy pan until the butter melts.

Add the sugar and stir over low heat until dissolved. Raise the heat
and bring to the boil. Without stirring, let the mixture cook at a slow
rolling boil until it reaches the soft ball stage (114°C/238°F on a sugar
thermometer). This will take about 10 minutes.

Remove the pan from the heat and add the condensed milk and
honey. Return to the heat, stirring, for a few minutes. Remove from the
heat, add the vanilla extract, and beat with a wooden spoon until the
mixture is glossy. Pour into the tin, then leave to cool.

Cut into cubes and store in an airtight tin. Place in petits fours cases
to serve.

HONEY-SESAME CRUNCH

These are wholesome and energizing little confections. Densely packed with sesame seeds and lightly sweetened with honey and brown sugar, they make a great afternoon pick-me-up.

Makes about 400g/14oz

*butter and grapeseed or
    groundnut (peanut) oil, for
    greasing*
*100g/3¾oz/8 tbsp soft light
    brown sugar*
*100ml/3½fl oz/scant ½ cup
    honey*
200g/7oz raw sesame seeds

VARIATIONS
• Try mixing different seeds into the mixture. Flax seeds are a good source of omega oils and taste delicious.
• For a sweet and tangy version, add 25g/1oz finely chopped dried apricots with the sesame seeds.

Per total amount: Energy 1878kcal/7850kJ; Protein 37.3g; Carbohydrate 182.7g, of which sugars 181.7g; Fat 116g, of which saturates 16.6g; Cholesterol 0mg; Calcium 1398mg; Fibre 15.8g; Sodium 57mg.

Grease a baking sheet with butter and set aside. Grease a rolling pin with oil.

Combine the sugar and honey in a small, heavy pan and place over a low heat, stirring constantly, to emulsify.

Add the raw sesame seeds and stir for about 10 minutes until the seeds are golden-brown.

Pour the mixture out on to the prepared baking sheet and run the oiled rolling pin over it to smooth the surface and attain a thickness of about 5mm/¼in.

Leave to cool slightly, but cut it into pieces while it is still warm or it will be too brittle and may shatter. Once cooled, keep in an airtight container or wrap each piece individually.

INDEX